W9-BXO-995   N LINE

BASEBALL HALL OF FAMERS

Lou Gehrig

Robert Greenberger

the rosen publishing group's
rosen
central

For Robbie, who helps me keep score and shares
a love for our national pastime

Published in 2004 by The Rosen Publishing Group, Inc.

29 East 21st Street, New York, NY 10010

Library of Congress Cataloging-in-Publication Data

Greenberger, Robert.
Lou Gehrig/by Robert Greenberger—1st ed.
    p. cm.—(Baseball Hall of Famers)
Summary: Discusses the personal life and baseball career of the
famous Yankee first baseman, Lou Gehrig.
Includes bibliographical references and index.
ISBN 0-8239-3781-X (lib. bdg.)
1.Gehrig, Lou, 1903-1941—Juvenile literature. 2.Baseball players—
United States—Biography—Juvenile literature. [1.Gehrig, Lou,1903-
1941. 2.Baseball players.]
I. Title. II. Series.
GV865.G4 G74 2003
796.352'092—dc21

Manufactured in the United States of America

2002010757

Contents

In 1936, Lou Gehrig led the American League in home runs and runs scored while playing for the Yankees.

Introduction

Lou Gehrig lived the American dream. Although he was a poor son of immigrants, he later developed athletic talents and became one of the greatest baseball players of all time.

While some players make history for their antics on the field, others are remembered for varied accomplishments. Lou Gehrig, recalled as a person who exhibited quiet grace and personal integrity, was one such athlete.

Though he is often remembered for his monumental output as a Yankee first baseman—with an amazing streak of 2,130 consecutive games played—when he was fatally diagnosed with amyotrophic lateral sclerosis (later known as Lou Gehrig's disease), Gehrig stood out as an example of courageousness to people everywhere.

A view of Broadway from Dey Street in New York City, around the year 1900. This was the New York of Lou Gehrig's childhood.

An Immigrant's Life

At the beginning of the twentieth century, America was seen as a land of opportunity. As conflicts in Europe grew, later compounding into World War I, thousands traveled to the United States in search of a better life. Immigrants came from all over the world and lived in neighborhoods thick with their fellow countrymen.

Christina Fack, fresh from Germany, came to live in the Yorkville section of New York when she was eighteen years old. Once there, she met Heinrich Gehrig, a sociable, German-born man who had arrived in America eleven years earlier, in 1888. Within a year, the couple began dating. They married in 1900. Later, they began raising a family.

Though Heinrich lacked a strong work ethic, he worked at a variety of jobs. His best skills were those of a metal artist, pounding tiny holes in sheet metal. Jobs were infrequent, however, and Heinrich's lackluster work ethic combined with his chronic poor health often kept him unemployed. Financial support for the family fell to Christina, who also ran the household.

Sadness and Strength

Two years after they married, the Gehrigs started a family. Tragically, the couple's first child, Sophie, died from diphtheria in 1906. Their next child, Anna, also died little more than a year later, shortly before their third child, an unnamed son, died just after being born. It isn't surprising that when the couple's fourth child, Henry Louis Gehrig II, was born on June 19, 1903, Christina would feel compelled to watch over him. Mother and son quickly formed a lasting bond.

It never dawned on Louis, as he was called, that his parents were poor. Christina did laundry, cleaned houses, and cooked. She was a highly motivated woman, and her behavior instilled similar values in her son. In fact, his earliest memories involved helping his mother deliver

During Louis's childhood, working-class women like his mother Christina often worked in laundries, as depicted in this advertisement from the era.

laundry. All earnings went into a glass jar safely kept in the kitchen.

Christina, bold by nature, raised Louis with a firm hand. Louis learned such a sense of responsibility that when he was once kept home from school with a fever, he snuck out of the house and attended class anyway. When the school's principal saw him, he recognized that Louis belonged at home, though Gehrig argued that he wanted to attend class.

Louis's father, Heinrich, was inattentive, spending much of his free time at a turnverein, a type of gymnasium, or at the local pub playing pinochle, then a popular card game. When Heinrich did observe his growing, pudgy son, he didn't quite understand the various pastimes that the boy enjoyed. When Heinrich bought Louis a catcher's mitt for Christmas, he didn't know that his son was a left-handed player and the mitt was designed only for right-handed children.

In those days, children woke as early as 5 AM, playing in the streets before school started. Whenever Louis wasn't helping his mother, he played. Later, Louis became a talented football player, though he was also captivated by baseball. Like most other German boys in his neighborhood, Louis never thought twice when he was called Heinie or Kraut-head, especially since he called his friends by similar nicknames.

But things changed when Louis turned five years old and he and his family moved from Yorkville to Washington Heights. Christina believed the new home was better located for a growing boy, with more room to

Children gather in a New York City playground at the turn of the century.

play. What she failed to consider, however, were the changes in ethnicity—the new neighborhood's block was largely home to Irish and Hungarian families—and suddenly Louis was being called a Heinie more as an ethnic slur than as an affectionate nickname.

Still, Louis grew up in this environment and became a strong, well-adjusted teenager. When Heinrich noticed his son's budding strength, he began taking him to his gym to help him develop a stronger upper body.

Hard Times

Growing up was sometimes difficult for Louis, who frequently wore hand-me-down clothing. He learned to endure the harsh New York winters without an overcoat, an item that he never owned until he was an adult. Hardships did not deter Louis from becoming a good student, though. He also had a series of part-time jobs that brought in much-needed money for his family. These positions included working as a deli clerk, running errands, mowing lawns, shoveling snow, and collecting money for the New York Edison Company (known later as Consolidated Edison, or Con Ed). Louis even went clamming, often selling his catch to local restaurants.

While most of his classmates did not continue studying beyond primary school, Christina was determined that her son receive a higher education. When his family moved again, now downtown to Greenwich Village, Louis continued to work, study, and play ball. He enrolled in the High School of Commerce in Manhattan so he could learn a trade. While his

Columbia University as it looked in the early 1900s. Gehrig attended Columbia, but he never felt accepted there because of his working-class background.

thick fingers clumsily fought manual typewriters, they more easily gripped a football. With little effort, Louis became an athlete.

Bobby Watt, head of Columbia University's Sigma Nu chapter, hired Christina Gehrig as a house cook while Louis, now known as Lou, studied. It meant a long commute for Christina, but the rate of pay and the appreciation that she gained from the young men of Sigma Nu was well worth it.

Gehrig, now more than six feet tall, was a member of his school's football team, though part-time jobs frequently made him late for practice. Once tardy and covered in soot, he had to explain that he needed to cover his father's duties as a janitor because Heinrich was ill.

Early Moments

In 1917, Gehrig played in his first school baseball game. Upon hearing about Gehrig's talents, the teacher and coach had insisted that Gehrig try out for the team.

By 1919, Gehrig, eager to help his family, found work with the Otis Elevator Company and joined their company baseball team. It wasn't until he played with the Minqua Baseball Club, a semiprofessional team, however that Gehrig was paid for his athletic ability. He either pitched or caught since those players were guaranteed $5 each; position players received less.

In June 1920, the Commerce High team was chosen to represent New York City in a championship against Lane Tech in Chicago.

Sponsored by the *New York Daily News*, Coach Harry Kane was allowed to bring nine boys on the trip, including Gehrig. His parents refused permission at first for Lou to play in the game. Kane had to make a personal appeal to Christina, promising he'd personally watch her son.

The trip was a series of firsts for Gehrig, who had never traveled to a different city, taken a long-distance train ride, or eaten expensive meals. On the trip west, a variety of notables visited the team, including former president William Howard Taft, then a justice on the U.S. Supreme Court.

The ballgame was a close affair, but in the ninth inning, Gehrig came to bat with the bases full and with two outs. He hit a grand slam, putting the game out of reach of the local team. The final score was 12–6, and the New York team reached celebrity status. It was the first time the newspapers compared Gehrig to Babe Ruth, then the reigning superstar in professional baseball.

That summer, Gehrig spent time working alongside his father, though he much preferred playing sports to performing manual labor.

Certifiable Talent

One of the first people to single Gehrig out from his teammates was Bobby Watt, a player returning to Columbia University, his alma mater, from World War I as graduate manager of athletics in 1919. In the fall of 1920, he was asked if the South Field could be used for the annual football game between Commerce High and De Witt Clinton High School. After he approved the use of the field, he stuck around to watch the contest. Later, Christina found him on the field and asked what he thought of Lou's ability. Watt hadn't connected the husky running back with the same boy who helped his mom at the fraternity house.

Seeing how he had grown, Watt worked with Columbia's football coach Frank "Buck" O'Neill to convince Gehrig to play for the university. Gehrig later admitted that two dozen various schools were vying for his talents, but Watt made the strongest pitch. Although Christina was worried about her son leaving home, he was convinced that playing ball for Columbia would be a wonderful opportunity.

Gehrig agreed to attend Columbia in February 1921. He then spent the next few months at the university's extension department, completing the credits required for his attendance as a college freshman that autumn.

The Minor Leagues

That summer, though, Gehrig got into trouble, almost jeopardizing his amateur athlete status. Arthur Irwin, a scout for the legendary New York Giants, convinced Gehrig to play professional ball. Irwin arranged for Gehrig to report to the Polo Grounds to practice with the Giants so that legendary manager John McGraw could evaluate his talents. Gehrig was instead on the sidelines for three days while McGraw growled that he had no time to develop a rookie, given his team's obvious slump.

Art Devlin, a former Giants third baseman, pulled Gehrig aside and suggested that he get some playing time in the minor leagues. He offered to arrange for Gehrig to play for the

This photograph shows Gehrig in May 1923, when he was already a rising star playing baseball for Columbia University in New York City.

Hartford team. To protect his amateur status, he would need to play under an assumed name, but Devlin and Irwin assured Gehrig that this was normal. Very naïvely, Gehrig agreed.

On June 3, 1921, Lou "Lewis" began playing for the Hartford Senators. His stint lasted for a mere dozen games, but he posted an impressive .261 average with two triples and one double.

Art Coakley, Columbia's baseball coach, heard what Gehrig was up to and traveled 130 miles north of New York City just to bring his prospect home. Gehrig denied knowingly breaking the rules, but something would now have to be done to preserve his ability to play at all while attending Columbia.

Watt appealed to the school's administration, suggesting that Gehrig was misled by scouts. Ultimately, Gehrig's punishment would be his ineligibility to play football or baseball during his freshman year. As a result, Gehrig watched longingly from the sidelines for the next two semesters.

2 A Budding Sports Star

Lou Gehrig spent his first year on the bench, watching games with football coach Buck O'Neill. Although Gehrig had played halfback at Commerce High, O'Neill wanted him to become a lineman. Both men eventually compromised, and Gehrig was used in various positions as a sophomore player.

Gehrig also decided to play some semiprofessional baseball to stay sharp and earn money, this time for a Morristown, New Jersey, team. He played under the name Lou Long, but since these were a few weekend games, everyone turned a blind eye to the activity.

University Life

Soon Gehrig was a fraternity pledge, though not at Sigma Nu, where his mother continued to cook, but at Phi Delta Theta. A dutiful son, Lou would help his mother while also waiting tables. Much as he grew to dislike his Washington Heights neighborhood, Gehrig was also unhappy with the snobbish ways at Columbia. Columbia is a prestigious university, as it was when Gehrig attended. Some of Gehrig's peers made it clear to him that he wasn't good enough to be a student there. In later years, he avoided approaches by his alumni association, making infrequent appearances there as a professional athlete.

Gehrig pitched in his only season with the Columbia Lions, striking out 17 players in a single game, which was a record. During the season, Coach Coakley used Gehrig as pitcher and an outfielder.

Yankee scout Paul Krichell ran into Coakley on a train as the team returned from playing Cornell University. The coach talked up this big kid who would be a great pitcher. At this suggestion, Krichell agreed to watch Gehrig play. Krichell arrived on Thursday, April 26, and was informed that Gehrig wasn't going to pitch that day. But Krichell stayed to watch anyway. Later

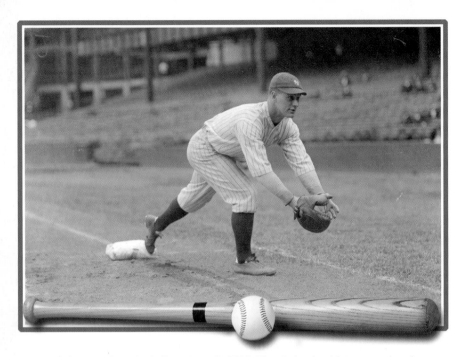

Gehrig catches the ball on June 5, 1923. The Columbia University player's great season made him a contender to join the legendary New York Yankees.

he recalled, as written in Ray Robinson's book *Iron Horse: Lou Gehrig in His Time*, "I did not go there to look at Gehrig. I did not even know what position he played. But . . . I sat up and took notice [anyway]. I saw a tremendous youth, with powerful arms and terrific legs. I said . . . Here is a kid who can't miss."

The following day, Krichell approached Ed Barrow, the Yankees' general manager, and insisted they sign Gehrig, though Barrow asked Krichell to check out another game to be certain. On April 28, Gehrig smacked a single and a homer, convincing Krichell that the young man should be a Yankee.

Becoming a Yankee

After the game, Krichell found Gehrig in the locker room. The mere mention of the New York Yankees to Gehrig, a kid who had grown up near the team, was all it took to capture his attention. A meeting was arranged the following day.

Nervous and feeling out of place, Gehrig brought his coach along to meet with Krichell and Barrow. Gehrig was offered $2,000 to play for the remaining four months of the 1923 baseball season, plus a $1,500 signing bonus. In those days, it was a good offer. As the contract was being drawn, Christina was home with double pneumonia, one of the rare times she was ever sick, and his father needed an operation. College would have to wait while he played ball as a pro.

In May, he reported to the stadium for the first time and met Miller Huggins, the stern manager of the team. Huggins interrupted batting practice to let Gehrig take some swings. The players were impressed that the manager himself was escorting Gehrig, a rookie, to the field. Yankee teammates appraised the muscular fellow while he reached down and grabbed a bat. Without realizing it, Gehrig selected one of Babe Ruth's prize forty-eight-ounce sticks. Soon Gehrig replaced first baseman Wally Pipp in the batter's box.

Although he missed the first few pitches, Gehrig soon started to make contact, hitting a few balls into the infield. He then cranked one into the right field bleachers, a feat previously accomplished only by the Babe.

Several months passed. When Gehrig joined the team that season, Huggins kept him close, explaining the intricacies of strategy to him until he finally played in an official game. He saw no action. By this time, his father's operation had been successful and Christina had recovered. Delighted, they both began to attend ball games, although neither understood how it was played. They were dismayed to see their son get paid to sit on a bench.

Learning to Play Ball

It was soon clear that Lou Gehrig needed additional training. Despite his obvious skills as a first baseman, his reaction time was poor and he was heavy-footed, sometimes unsure where to throw the ball. The team, fond of nicknames, dubbed him Tanglefoot.

Huggins explained to Gehrig that he was being optioned to Hartford, Connecticut, of all places, to gain additional experience. The Senators then had a relationship with the Yankees, and Huggins's former coach, Paddy O'Connor, was the manager. Not thrilled, but dutiful, Gehrig went back to Connecticut.

O'Connor was hard on the team, especially on Gehrig. His first two weeks as a Senator were miserable. In frustration, O'Connor sent a telegram to Barrow, asking him to take the player back. Confused, Barrow got in touch with Krichell, then scouting in

South Carolina, before heading north to Connecticut to determine what was wrong.

Krichell arrived to see Gehrig play. Afterwards, he invited a dejected Gehrig to dinner where they talked. Gehrig had difficulty accepting anything other than perfection from his game and Krichells' impression was that Gehrig's fear of failure was strong.

Making the Grade

Gehrig finally began hitting the ball with authority later that summer. He played in 59 games and hit .304. His confidence was renewed, and Harry Hesse, the first baseman he had displaced to the outfield, fixed Gehrig up on his first date. Gehrig was shy and awkward, and the outing went poorly, but it was a milestone nonetheless.

By late September, Huggins brought Gehrig back to the Yankees now that the team had clinched the American League pennant. Regular first baseman Wally Pipp had hurt his ankle, so Gehrig made another start. This time he hit his first major league home run off the Boston Red Sox's "Wild Bill" Piercy.

Gehrig (*right*) soon took his place beside his superstar teammate Babe Ruth (*left*) and manager Miller Huggins (*center*). Here they appear during spring training in 1929.

Jacob "Colonel" Ruppert, the owner of the Yankees, appealed to baseball commissioner Kenesaw Mountain Landis to allow Gehrig to play on the World Series Yankees squad even though he joined after the September 1 deadline. Landis said it was fine with him if the National League champion Giants agreed. Giants Manager John McGraw, recalling Gehrig's abilities, refused. Even without Gehrig, the Yankees beat the Giants anyway.

Life as a Rookie

In February 1924, Gehrig reported to the Yankees' spring training camp in New Orleans. He was excited to be working out with the team, hoping to become a regular. Pipp was especially gracious, taking time to teach his potential replacement the subtleties of playing first base.

Gehrig's greatest problem was a financial one. To make ends meet, he still took odd jobs that winter. At one point, he had only $14 in his pocket. Huggins arranged for him to room with rookie catcher Benny Bengough, since he had little cash for private accommodations.

Still, being a rookie was tough in other ways. The veteran players crowded Gehrig and others out of batting practice. Huggins had Coach Charley O'Leary meet with Gehrig at 10 AM, an hour before practice, to work on his batting technique.

That spring, Gehrig continued to improve as a fielder, and his hitting remained impressive. Since Pipp was still the regular first baseman, Gehrig knew he'd once again start the season

A Short History of the New York Yankees

The New York Yankees grew from the remnants of the Baltimore Orioles when Frank Farell and Bill Devery bought the team and moved them north in 1905. They

The almost-built Yankee Stadium in 1923

played their first games at an all-wood ballpark at 168th Street and Broadway. Because of the ballpark's elevation, the team was called the Highlanders, and their stadium was dubbed Hilltop Park. They played their first game on April 22, 1903, losing to the Washington Senators, 3–1.

In 1912, the now famous pinstripes were added to the uniforms, and their name became the Yankees in April 1913. That year, they relocated to the Polo Grounds in the Bronx, also home to the New York Giants.

Things did not improve for the franchise until Jacob Ruppert and Tillinghast L'Hommedieu Huston purchased the team for $460,000 in January 1915. They finally got a winner when they acquired Babe Ruth from the Boston Red Sox in 1920. His price of $125,000 and a $350,000 loan was considered a steal for the team, especially when they won their first pennant in 1921. The following year they built Yankee Stadium—designed in part to take advantage of Ruth's power swing. When it opened a year later, it was quickly dubbed "The House that Ruth Built."

riding the bench. Instead, Huggins summoned Gehrig to his hotel room just before the team headed north to begin the season. Huggins said Gehrig was being optioned back to Hartford, Connecticut, not because he didn't measure up, but because he needed to play every day— something he could not do with the big league team. Huggins promised that when Gehrig returned in the fall, he would be back to stay.

Gehrig started the 1924 season with the team, notching just a dozen pinch-hit appearances before returning to Hartford. Determined to prove that Huggins's confidence was properly placed, Gehrig hit .369 in 134 games that summer. He also committed 23 errors at first base, something Huggins and his staff would later help him correct.

Gehrig was recalled, as promised, in September. Injuries to a few players and an aging roster meant the team's chance at a fourth straight pennant was unlikely. The season ended quietly, and Gehrig returned home knowing he was finally a professional ballplayer.

Murderer's Row

T he Yankees changed locations, and in 1925, spring training was held in Fort Lauderdale, Florida. The team made some trades, hoping to improve in a few areas, but none of the moves made room for Lou Gehrig. He still worked out with the team, and Wally Pipp continued to instruct him on the nuances of playing first base. Finally, Gehrig played with a steady confidence.

Although no one knew it at the time, the Yankees were in for a rocky season. Babe Ruth—"the Sultan of Swat"—was waylaid with a stomach ailment that kept him out of the lineup for months. As a result, the team faltered and couldn't recover.

On June 1, the Babe returned. Though it turned out to be too soon, he played to a great ovation. As a result, few noticed that later in the game, Gehrig was summoned to pinch-hit for

Gehrig brings one home against the Chicago White Sox, his third home run of the game, on May 5, 1929.

Pee Wee Wanninger. His first appearance began the streak that helped Gehrig secure a place in baseball history.

Making Strides

The following day, during practice, Pipp was struck in the head with a baseball. Huggins decided to rest his aging, now-injured veteran. Gehrig started the game instead. He went three for five and performed so well that Huggins kept him in the lineup.

Gehrig hit .295 for the season, with 21 homers. He was thrilled to see his pal Benny Bengough behind the plate, another new face. None of the changes were good enough to put the Yankees in first place, though. The Babe was ailing, and the Yankees were out of the running for the second season in a row.

On June 24, Gehrig reached another milestone—his first stolen base. It was the first time anyone had stolen home plate as his first stolen base. Stealing home was a feat he would repeat fifteen times during his career. Over time, he would team with other players to perfect the double steal with Gehrig usually in the lead and stealing home.

Along the way, he continued to polish his performance. Off the field, he was absorbing information from Huggins and Ruth. It was Ruth, for example, who worked with Gehrig on where exactly to hit the ball. They were constant companions.

During the Off-Season

Gehrig was overjoyed at the idea of playing baseball regularly, so much so that he continued to play after the games ended. Gehrig often expressed his love for the sport by playing stickball with local kids.

Just after the season ended, Gehrig participated in a promotional stunt. He was joined by Leo Diegel, the Canadian Open golf champion; Paul Crouch, the champion archer; and Edwin Harkins, the champion rod-and-line man. They played nine holes of golf using their equipment: bat and ball, bow and arrow, golf

Gehrig takes another kind of swing during a golf game.

ball and club, and rod and line. Gehrig won by a stroke, taking home $250. When the stunt was repeated in 1927, he placed second.

Between seasons, Gehrig moved his mother and father into a new home in Morningside Heights, near Columbia University. By this time, Christina was accompanying her son to spring training. She continued to do so for the next decade. It was her six-week vacation, and Lou treated her like a queen.

Again, Yankee management made changes, hoping to revitalize the team. Ed Barrow and Miller Huggins brought up shortstop Mark Koenig and second baseman Tony Lazzeri. This third spring training for Gehrig was a turning point; he was no longer the raw, inept rookie. He had proven himself and had shown both power and ability. Huggins repeatedly pointed to Gehrig's character and said he led the team with his maturity.

Making His Mark

In 1926, the Yankees began to play well together, regaining their championship form. Gehrig continued to hit for power with 47 doubles, 20 triples, and 107 RBIs. He hit third, ahead of Ruth, making the most potent combination in any batting order and putting outright fear into pitchers from opposing teams. Behind them was Bob Meusel in the fifth spot, helping to form what was then called "Murderer's Row." The original nickname was used for a lineup of proven batters, including Ruth, but this grouping was even more dangerous.

The Yankees regained the American League pennant only to lose the World Series to the St. Louis Cardinals.

By now, Gehrig had gotten himself in a routine that included taking extra fielding practice. He recognized that he did not respond quickly enough to situational plays and that his slow reaction time might cost the team a game. No other Yankee player worked as hard to improve himself. Being merely a good player was never enough for Gehrig; he wanted greatness.

This first full season of play also meant he started collecting the bangs and bruises that would mark his career. Gehrig avoided having X rays taken during routine physicals because he feared that doctors would find an injury or fracture that might mean sitting on the bench. He had no intention of sitting down if he could play the game.

For the 1927 season, Huggins expected a better performance from the team and got it. This lineup was, and is still, considered by many to be the best Yankee team of all time. Every player did his best, but it was Murderer's Row—Ruth,

(l-r) Murderer's Row—Combs, Ruth, and Meusel

Gehrig, and Meusel—that propelled the team to an easy pennant. Gehrig set an RBI record with 175; it was the same season Ruth set the home run mark with 60, and the team won 110 games.

Gehrig not only hit well, but he also showed excellent defensive skills as a first baseman, proving that his extra effort was worthwhile. He even took the time to count the paces from first base to the field boxes at other ballparks, committing to memory the distance available to grab pop flies.

On the Road

Christy Walsh was Ruth's business manager and publicist, and he conceived the idea of a barnstorming tour. Together, they convinced Gehrig to join them. On October 11, the twenty-one-game, nine-state tour began. The "Bustin' Babes" and "Larrupin' Lous" were composed of local athletes playing alongside the legendary Yankees. They averaged 10,000 fans per stop, earning Gehrig more money in a month than he had earned in the entire 1927 season. They traveled through the southern states and west throughout California, where San Jose schools closed in honor of the event.

It was perhaps the closest Ruth and Gehrig ever were to one another, especially since their backgrounds were so different. Ruth was generous with his cash, spending extravagantly. In contrast, Gehrig, raised to be frugal, always worried about money.

Along the way, Ruth coached Gehrig on negotiating techniques for the upcoming winter

The Bustin' Babes and Lou Gehrig, who captained the opposing Larrupin Lous

contract talks. In 1927, Gehrig earned a mere $8,000, so Ruth suggested that he ask for $30,000. The suggestion shocked Gehrig, but he nodded. Weeks later, Ruth was angered to read that Gehrig had signed a two-year contract for $50,000. Though it became the first rift between the two players, it was not the last. Shortly afterward, Gehrig bought a house for himself and his parents north of the Bronx in New Rochelle, in the Westchester suburbs.

The team virtually repeated themselves in 1928, although they had to fend off the Philadelphia Athletics by season's end. Gehrig hit several home runs during the World Series, hitting four of the team's nine.

It should be noted that, during the World Series, Gehrig met Eleanor Twitchell, who would later become his love interest. Although the introduction didn't leave an impression on Gehrig, several years later, in 1932, both remembered the brief exchange.

A Winning Team

The Yankees continued to smack the ball with authority. Joe Shaute of the Cleveland Indians was pitching against Murderer's Row, hoping they would hit to the left instead of into the short right-field fence at League Park. Instead, Ruth smacked a liner that hit third baseman Rube Lutzke on the shoulder. Next, Gehrig lined one into Lutzke's shin. Bob Meusel's subsequent drive hit Lutzke in the stomach. "Why, a guy would have been safer in the first World War!"

Ruth and Gehrig both make it home during a September 1928 game.

Lutzke said after the game, as recounted in the Frank Graham book, *Lou Gehrig, a Quiet Hero*.

Gehrig had matured as a player, improving at the first-base position and continuing to be a fine example to the rest of the team. He spoke infrequently, but when he did it was sincere. In reality, Gehrig was uncomfortable around other people. He never mastered much social grace and was normally too busy working or playing ball to make small talk.

Baseball in Gehrig's Day

Baseball traces its roots to the early 1800s, although the actual birth of the game has remained a cause for speculation. The legend of Abner Doubleday as its creator has been debunked, but he did help to popularize baseball.

When Gehrig joined the Yankees in 1925, there were two leagues, American and National. There were only eight teams in each league and there were no divisions. Many cities—New York, Boston, St. Louis, and Philadelphia—boasted one team in each league. The season lasted 154 games, from late April through the end of September, with the pennant winners meeting in the World Series.

During Gehrig's tenure, the Baseball Hall of Fame was opened in 1938 and the All-Star Game was introduced. Baseball was predominantly a segregated sport, although Latin Americans and Native Americans played on several teams. Integration with African Americans did not occur in baseball until Jackie Robinson joined the Brooklyn Dodgers in 1947. The Boston Red Sox became the last American League team to integrate players of all races in the 1950s.

Gehrig signs autographs for a few gleeful young fans in the 1940s.

Still, Gehrig took his place as a role model seriously. For instance, he was never photographed while holding a pipe or a cigarette, though he did smoke regularly. Gehrig seemed more comfortable with children than with his own peers. When a window was broken during one of his stickball games, police recognized Gehrig and complimented him, but asked that they knock off the games to preserve the peace. Reluctantly, Gehrig agreed.

5 Lineup Changes

The happy post–World War I days came to an end with the October stock market crash in 1929, sending the country into a prolonged economic slowdown known as the Great Depression. The year proved to be a period of changes for America, including reforms for the New York Yankees. Batting averages plunged shortly before stock prices fell, and, as a result, the team was struggling to stay atop the league that August.

A Great Loss

Teammate and manager Miller Huggins suffered right beside his peers, seemingly tired and pained by their woeful performance. On September 20, Huggins needed help suiting up for the game. He lasted just three innings and was then taken to St.

Vincent's Hospital. Huggins died just five days later, suffering from erysipelas, a rare and fatal skin disease.

Gehrig was devastated by the loss. Huggins had stuck by Gehrig, always encouraging him to improve his game. "Only Lou's willingness and lack of conceit will make him into a complete ball player. That and those muscles are all he has," Huggins had said, according to the Web site www.baseball-almanac.com.

Huggins's death seemed to sap any spirit left in the Yankees, and they lost the pennant to Connie Mack's Philadelphia Athletics, who went on to win the World Series.

During the off-season, Gehrig tried his hand at stock trading by joining the Wall Street firm of Appenfellar, Allen, and Hill. His tenure was brief, and he quickly found that he did not have the instincts required for the fast-paced world of high finance.

Growing Pains

After the last season, changes were required in the Yankee's lineup. Ed Barrow made some

Gehrig checks the stock ticker at the trading firm Appenfellar, Allen, and Hill during his brief stint as a stock broker in the off-season of 1929.

roster moves, including trading Bob Meusel, one of the "murderers." Other older players were also being traded, while rookie players were joining the ranks. Still, the team didn't seem to resemble the force it once was. The biggest Yankee news of the day was the team's new manager, Bob Shawkey, a former Red Sox and Yankees pitcher.

The team wasn't sure what to make of their new skipper, but they were all professionals.

Claire Ruth, the Babe's second wife, said in the John Tullius book *I'd Rather Be a Yankee*, "From the beginning, he [Gehrig] was simply a gorgeous hitter. My husband's long drives were much like his swing—gracefully arching balls that seemed to flow from a bat that, in turn, was flowing effortlessly, propelled by a gracefully twisting body.

"Lou [Gehrig] hit that ball like a Mack truck running into a stone wall at 100 miles per hour. You could see mighty muscles tensing and exploding under his taut uniform. He personified power, and his line drives literally screeched as they headed for the outfield or the bleachers."

New Leadership

Shawkey kept the Yankees competing, going neck and neck with the Cleveland Indians. The Yanks' efforts were not enough, though, and the Athletics remained both American League and world champions. Owner Jacob Ruppert had seen enough. He felt that the team needed a different manager. During the World Series, the Chicago Cubs fired their manager, Joe McCarthy. Ruppert then zeroed in on him as his top choice to manage the Yankees' future.

McCarthy welcomed the team during spring training in 1931, and, once again, the Yanks warmed up to their new leader. Gehrig and catcher Bill Dickey, then roommates, both liked McCarthy's no-nonsense style. McCarthy demanded the best from his players and no score was high enough. He had strict rules on and off the field, and Gehrig responded favorably to his instruction. Ruth, on the other hand, fretted under the restrictions but did the best he could.

McCarthy quickly earned Gehrig's trust and came to admire the quiet first baseman. He

Joe McCarthy *(far left)* became the Yankees' manager in 1931. Gehrig, standing next to McCarthy, is seen with the other Yankee members of the American League all-star team of 1938.

became Gehrig's new mentor, which inspired him to continue his excellent performance. "I had him for over eight years and he never gave me a moment's trouble," McCarthy said in the Robinson book *Iron Horse.* "I guess you might say he was kind of my favorite."

Missed Opportunities

It was another season of home runs for Ruth and Gehrig, tying at 46 for the home run record.

Gehrig would have won with 47, had shortstop Lyn Lary not committed an error early in the season. Lary was on first when Gehrig smacked a homer and thought the ball might have been caught. Rather than round third base and head for home plate, he headed from third to the dugout. Gehrig, head down, didn't notice the mistake and was called out for passing another runner on the base path and was credited with a triple, costing him the homer.

Despite hitting 184 RBIs, Gehrig was disturbed to see his average slump from .379 in 1930 to .341 in 1931. He begged people to tell him what he was doing wrong. Although .341 would be terrific for anyone else, it alarmed Gehrig.

The team still fell short that season, coming in second. McCarthy reassured Ruppert that he came to win, however, and was confident that they would the following year.

After the 1931 season, Gehrig joined a baseball all-star team that toured Japan. He found the people welcoming, impressed with the massive size of American ballplayers. Later,

Gehrig was said to have spent thousands of dollars on gifts for his mom while on the tour.

By this time, the Yankees had settled into their routine. Christina Gehrig's kitchen was busy as she hosted groups of her son's teammates. These groups became known as "Mom's Boys" and included, at one time or another, Babe Ruth, Benny Bengough, Bob Meusel, Joe Dugan, Tony Lazzeri, and Mark Koenig. Dorothy Ruth, Babe's daughter, was so friendly with Christina that the Gehrig family set aside a room in the Westchester home just for her use. By this time, Gehrig was busy with his own home, which had turned into a menagerie. He was an animal lover, and his house now contained a parrot, two canaries, and two dogs.

As promised, McCarthy led the Yankees to victory, retaking the American League crown from the Athletics in 1932.

"Home Run Game"

The absolute highlight of the season had to have been Gehrig's "home run game." On June 3, 1932,

Gehrig managed three consecutive homers into right field off the Philadelphia Athletics pitcher George "Moose" Earnshaw. When Gehrig next came to bat, Athletics manager Connie Mack withdrew Earnshaw from the game, but invited him to stay on the bench to see what another pitcher, Leroy Mahaffey, could do with Gehrig. During that seventh inning, Gehrig smacked his fourth homer—into left field. "I understand now, Mr. Mack," Earnshaw said, according to Richard Hubler's book *Lou Gehrig: The Iron Horse of Baseball.* "Mahaffey made Lou change his direction. Can I shower now?"

Just before the game ended, Gehrig narrowly missed a fifth home run when Al Simmons snatched the ball just on the other side of the fence.

Unfortunately for Gehrig, it was also the same day that John McGraw retired from managing the Giants, ending a thirty-year career. News of McGraw's retirement—and not of Gehrig's home run game—made the morning headlines.

By now, everyone on the Yankees had a routine, including Gehrig, who had long since established the habit of chewing gum and smoothing the dirt around first base with his bare hand. The club trainer, Doc Painter, said in Robinson's book *Iron Horse*, "My one duty with Gehrig is to see that he is supplied with chewing gum before the start of each game. At the beginning of the season he gives me money for a couple of cartons of the cud and I dole it out a stick at a time . . .

"Gehrig has lasted so long and held up wonderfully because he takes intelligent care of himself. While he doesn't pamper himself any, he doesn't let a minor injury go. Moreover, he follows his personal physician's advice religiously and pays particular attention to his diet. He sees to it that he gets the proper amount of sleep each night, too."

The Babe

The Yankees cruised to the World Series and traveled to Chicago to play the Cubs in one of the most memorable matchups of all time. During the game, the infamous "called shot" occurred, and to this day, people debate whether or not Babe Ruth actually predicted that his next hit would be a homer over the center field wall. Immediately after the game, Gehrig laughed and said, as it was written in a book by Bert Randolph Sugar, *Rain Delays*, "What do you think of the nerve of that big monkey? Imagine the guy calling his shot and getting away with it!"

In the off-season, *Liberty* magazine ran an article by Gehrig entitled "Am I Jealous of Babe Ruth?" The published answer was no, but it didn't always seem that way to his teammates.

In 1933, Dan Daniel of the *New York World-Telegraph* figured out that Gehrig, who prided himself on his dependability, was about to eclipse Everett Scott's 1,307 consecutive game record. By now, Ruth's career was starting to slow down.

The Streak

Gehrig tied Scott's record on August 16, getting two hits. He beat the record the following

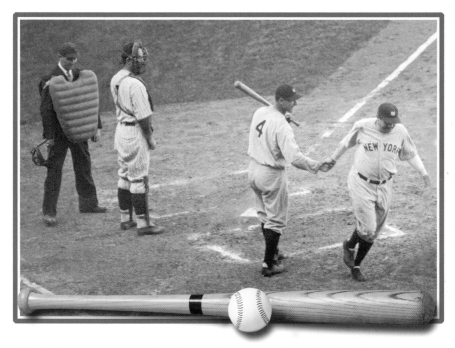

Babe Ruth crosses the plate after hitting a home run in Game 3 of the 1932 World Series. This was the famous homer that Ruth is rumored to have predicted by pointing his finger towards center field, indicating where he was going to hit the ball.

afternoon. Unfortunately, the Yankees lost, and Gehrig took no pleasure in his new record, despite getting two additional hits. The Yankees recorded the event after the first inning when Gehrig received an award from American League president Will Harridge. Scott, who was by then retired from the game, said he was glad that his record fell to his former teammate. (Yankee general manager Ed Barrow is said to have called a game—preserving Gehrig's streak—while Gehrig was in court with Christina regarding a traffic accident. Barrow claimed that he called the game because of bad weather, despite a cloudless sky.)

The closest time Gehrig came to missing a game was due to injuries. His back seized on him on July 13, 1934, and the following day he begged McCarthy to let him bat first in the game and then be replaced. Sure enough, Gehrig, listed atop the order as shortstop, smacked a single, trotted to first base, and came out for a pinch runner. By the next game, he was back in for good.

Despite not receiving as much press as Ruth, Gehrig had devoted fans around the country. When the first All-Star Game was played in 1933, he was overwhelmingly voted to start at first base, beating the Philadelphia Athletics' Jimmie Foxx by 185,576 votes.

Wedding Bells

Lou Gehrig always proclaimed that his mother was his best girl, but he had dated since his college days. In fact, in 1932, he was taken with a young woman he met during spring training. Christina Gehrig was in attendance, as usual, and reacted poorly to the notion of a new woman in her son's life.

During the 1932 World Series, Gehrig was in Chicago at a party where he was reintroduced to Eleanor Grace Twitchell. She remembered meeting him four years earlier, but was even more impressed with the handsome ball player this time. Gehrig was equally infatuated.

Eleanor Twitchell was born in 1905 and grew up in Chicago. Her father, Frank Bradford Twitchell, had a variety of careers, but unlike

Gehrig fell in love with Eleanor Twitchell in 1932, and they married in 1933. Here she sings to him at Leon and Eddie's night club in New York in 1935.

the Gehrigs, the Twitchell family was never in dire financial straits.

Since Gehrig had a curfew, the meeting between he and Eleanor was brief. Soon after, he sent her a gift—a diamond necklace that he had picked up while in Japan.

Making Plans

A courtship was underway. The pair spoke by phone and wrote letters. When the Yankees made their first trip to Chicago in 1933, people noticed sparks between the couple. It became obvious they would get married, although the actual proposal was difficult for Gehrig. He was so nervous about asking for her hand that he couldn't quite express himself. At last, Eleanor coaxed it out of him.

Once it became clear that the couple were to be married, Christina became concerned about her son. Even Gehrig admitted that his mother could be a handful, so Eleanor invited her future mother-in-law to Chicago for a visit. It did not go terribly well. Christina was critical of her son's lifestyle and the plans that he and Eleanor were making. Eventually, Lou had a chat with his mother to explain that he was making a life with Eleanor whether she liked it or not.

Afterward, Eleanor left Chicago and took an apartment near the Gehrig home. Over time, the two women formed a stiff relationship. The experience was straining on both Gehrig and Eleanor, but their love was strong.

A Quiet Ceremony

They set the wedding date for September 1933.
Rather than wait, Gehrig decided they'd get
married quietly, earlier than expected. Gehrig
called Walter G. C. Otto, mayor of New Rochelle,
New York, to come and perform the ceremony.
Witnessing the event were Fred Linder and
Eleanor's aunt, Blanche C. Austin. The laborers
scurrying around the Gehrigs' new home stopped
long enough to watch the event in respectful
silence. Champagne was passed around to all.

The mayor had a motorcycle escort ride
with Gehrig and Eleanor as they headed to the
Bronx for the afternoon game. Before game
time, Gehrig broke the happy news to the press
and his teammates, surprising Bill Dickey, who
thought he was invited to the event that
evening. In that night's game, the Yanks lost to
the Washington Senators and Gehrig went
hitless. The following day, there was a
reception for the couple at Eleanor's aunt's
home on Long Island, reluctantly attended by
Gehrig's mother, Christina.

This photo shows Gehrig and his bride on their wedding day, September 30, 1933, in New Rochelle, New York, surrounded by friends and family.

Once Gehrig announced to his mother that he had married, Christina began frequently commenting on the financial hardship that she and her husband might now endure. To settle the issue, Gehrig arranged to put all his savings in a trust that would provide a monthly income to his parents. He had already given them the deed to their house, so they were set for life. Christina could finally stop working.

The newlyweds began their married life with little money in the bank but with a great deal of promise for the future. Gehrig, after arranging for his parents' comfort, handed the checkbook to Eleanor, putting their financial future in her hands.

Beginnings and Endings

During the off-season, Eleanor began transforming Gehrig into a new man, outfitting him in fine tailored suits. Similarly, she began introducing him to the culture his upbringing never included, such as the opera, one of her loves. She took Gehrig to see a German opera, *Tristan and Isolde*. Quickly Gehrig became a major fan, repeatedly returning to opera houses and befriending performers.

Similarly, Gehrig introduced his wife to his favorite passions, including westerns, ice-skating, and fishing. As they learned more about each other, their love deepened. Eleanor called her husband Luke in public and Dracula or Monster in private, while he privately, and jokingly, called her Battleaxe and Old Bat.

Eleanor recalled these as the happiest days of her life. During these months, they decided that Lou would retire at age thirty-five, before becoming just another athlete with fading skills. What he would do after retirement was undetermined, but, whatever it was, they would do it together.

Obviously, Gehrig was pointedly trying to avoid what was happening to Babe Ruth. With each passing year, Ruth's power numbers were dropping as his weight was rising. It was also obvious that Yankee manager Joe McCarthy was beginning to build his team around Gehrig, and not around Ruth.

Spring training in 1934 was a new beginning for the Gehrigs, but also a year of endings. Eleanor had to leave early because her father was dying, and it was also obvious to Gehrig that the season was Ruth's last. Sadly, it would also be the end of their friendship.

During this time, Ruth and his second wife, Claire, took a trip, leaving daughter Dorothy with a maid. When Dorothy visited Christina, she seemed shabbily dressed. The next time Christina saw the Ruths, she voiced her opinion that the child was being neglected, possibly in favor of Julia, Claire's daughter from a previous marriage. Claire was offended by the comment and Ruth withdrew from Gehrig. The two former friends no longer spoke to each other.

Trouble in Japan

Despite the setback, the season went beautifully. Gehrig hit well, and Eleanor adjusted to being a baseball wife. There was one scary incident in June during an exhibition game in Norfolk, Virginia. Gehrig was hit in the head with a pitch. Even though he was diagnosed with a concussion, he wouldn't dream of missing a game. Instead, he pounded out three triples only to have the game called on account of rain, erasing the batting performance from the record books. Gehrig played so well during that season that he won the Triple Crown, leading the league in home runs, runs batted in, and batting average. The Yankees, though, finished second to the Detroit Tigers, and after the season ended, Babe Ruth was released from his contract, ending an era.

That fall, Gehrig and other Yankee players returned to Japan by ship. This time Gehrig brought his wife. When Gehrig couldn't find her on board one night, he panicked, thinking she might have fallen overboard. Instead, Eleanor had been invited to share caviar with Ruth in his stateroom, a meeting that led to unsubstantiated rumors about the pair. It was the last place Gehrig would have looked for her. The rift between the two sluggers now seemed wider than ever.

The trip became the honeymoon the Gehrigs had never had. The ball-playing was fun, but once that ended, they took in the sights and visited a number of countries. It was a magical time, but both could sense storm clouds gathering as they visited Europe.

After previously taking a depression-era pay cut, Gehrig received a $7,000 raise that brought his salary for the 1935 season up to $30,000. Also, McCarthy named Gehrig team captain, an honor no player had received since 1922.

Captain Lou

Despite a fresh beginning, Lou Gehrig could not lead his team to victory in 1935. The Yankees finished in second place for the third time, with Gehrig's batting average down to .329. In all respects, it was a quiet season.

The Gehrigs continued to revel in each other's interests. By this time, Eleanor had completed scrapbooks of her husband's accomplishments. His mother, Christina, had saved newspaper articles dating from her son's Commerce High win in Chicago, and when Eleanor discovered them, she finished the job.

Joe DiMaggio

The Yankees, seeking to protect Gehrig in the 1936 lineup, employed a charismatic hitter from the Pacific Coast League named Joe DiMaggio.

By 1936, center fielder Joe DiMaggio was the newest rising star of the Yankees' roster, and the press seemed to prefer him over the more reserved Gehrig.

Immediately, fans welcomed DiMaggio and his electrifying hitting prowess. Again, the press flocked to someone flashier than old, dependable Gehrig. The Iron Horse was someone they could count on, but his contributions made mediocre newspaper copy. DiMaggio, on the other hand, was handsome and young, and never minded the spotlight.

With DiMaggio batting behind Gehrig, the Yankees took the pennant and were returning to the World Series, this time against their rivals, the Giants. Gehrig shared the cover of *Time* magazine with opposing pitcher Carl Hubbell. The Yankees struggled but prevailed, winning in six games.

Heading to Hollywood

Publicist Christy Walsh, who added Gehrig to his roster of clients, decided that the baseball hero might make a good actor. When Johnny Weismuller was to be replaced as the lead in the *Tarzan* movie series, Walsh encouraged Gehrig to take a screen test. When the media broke the story, Walsh doled out every tidbit. Gehrig did pose in a loincloth for some publicity shots, but the studio decided not to use him after all. When word reached Tarzan creator Edgar Rice Burroughs, he sent Gehrig a telegram saying, "[I] have seen several pictures of you as Tarzan and paid about fifty dollars for newspaper clippings on the subject. I want to congratulate you on being a swell first baseman."

By spring, Gehrig had signed a one-picture deal with Principal Productions, a low-budget

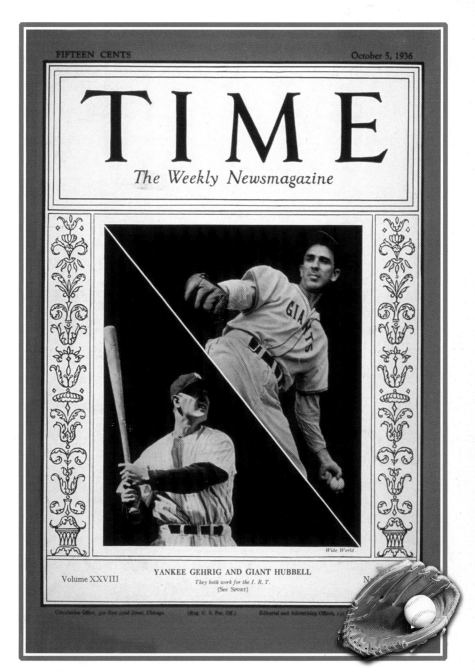

October 5, 1936

TIME

The Weekly Newsmagazine

Wide World

YANKEE GEHRIG AND GIANT HUBBELL

They both work for the I. R. T.

(See SPORT)

Volume XXVIII

Circulation Office, 350 East 22nd Street, Chicago.   (Reg. U. S. Pat. Off.)   Editorial and Advertising Offices, 135

World Series contenders Lou Gehrig and Carl Hubbell of the opposing New York Giants grace the October 5, 1936, issue of *Time* magazine.

Hollywood studio. They would develop a project to film after the 1937 season.

That winter, the Young Men's Board of Trade of New York honored Gehrig. He was the first athlete given the Distinguished Service Key for the example he set for the youth of New York City—something that made him very proud. Along the way, Gehrig also took a day to lecture at his alma mater, Columbia University. He was sometimes invited by the Teacher's College to speak to the crowded lecture hall.

In 1937, Gehrig, DiMaggio, and Dickey were the crucial trio in the lineup. They were not necessarily a "Murderer's Row," but opposing pitchers were concerned whenever they faced them. With their help, the team cruised to another pennant and another series against the Giants. It seemed like a repeat of 1936, although it took the Yankees five games, not six, to win. Gehrig homered off Hubbell in what proved to be his final postseason round-tripper.

During the winter, unlike his usually quiet self, Gehrig spent a great deal of time in

Hollywood, slightly caught up in his public lifestyle. He was taken to parties, dinners, and openings, and was photographed with several screen stars, though he refused to pose with starlets since he was a happily married man.

Filming *Rawhide* was a new experience for Gehrig, and after some practice he took to the part. He played himself, but it was a fabricated story that had him retire to his ranch after a salary dispute with the Yankees. He then got involved with rustlers and used his fists and steady throwing arm to protect the homestead. The female lead played his sister, saving Gehrig from having to share a screen kiss.

New Milestones

Gehrig, having lost the pounds he had gained in Hollywood, expected the Yankees to have another terrific year. He happily signed on for the new season with his salary reaching $39,000. DiMaggio, though, again stole the headlines with his demands for $45,000. When asked why he should be better paid than the Iron Horse, he

Gehrig jokes around on the set of *Rawhide* in Hollywood, California. He played a baseball-player-turned-cowboy who battles cattle rustlers.

reportedly told the general manager, as it was recounted in the Paul Dickson book *Baseball's Greatest Quotations*, "Mr. Barrow, there is only one answer to that—Mr. Gehrig is terribly underpaid."

Gehrig was approaching not only his thirty-fifth birthday, but also his 2,000th consecutive game. On the day he was scheduled to reach the milestone, Eleanor strongly suggested he instead sit the game out and let his record stand at 1,999. He never seriously considered her advice, feeling there was no reason to stop playing. She kidded him that all the Yankees would do was give him a horseshoe-shaped floral arrangement. Sure enough, he played and brought home the flowers.

Despite the highlight, it was Gehrig's worst season. His batting average plummeted into the .270s, and his power numbers were falling, too. Still, with DiMaggio, Dickey, and Tommy Henrich in the spotlight and scoring, the attention was off Gehrig, who ultimately had a terrible season. His slump ate away at him. He was further troubled by the fact that he had no idea what was holding his performance back.

The Yankees returned to the World Series anyway, this time facing the Chicago Cubs. Despite going 4 for 14, Gehrig's Yankees swept the Cubs in four games, taking their third series in a row. In fact, no team had won three in a row before 1938. Yankee manager McCarthy felt this team was the best one he had ever managed.

It was another quiet off-season for Gehrig and Eleanor, although storm clouds of an entirely different kind were starting to gather over their home in New Rochelle.

The Luckiest Man

8

Given his poor 1938 season, Lou Gehrig graciously accepted a $3,000 salary cut. He was determined to work harder than before and regain his winning form. It was a rough winter for Gehrig; he began stumbling while walking or ice-skating, for no apparent reason. Eleanor later admitted she never thought twice about what these sudden falls meant.

In a 1938 interview, reprinted in the Donald Honig book *Baseball: When the Grass Was Real*, McCarthy openly questioned Gehrig's ability to play baseball full-time. He hinted that either Babe Dahlgren or Tommy Henrich could be a replacement. It was the first sign of concern within the organization that the Iron Horse's days might be numbered.

The Yankees began the year losing then team owner Jacob Ruppert, who died at sixty-seven. His estate named Yankee president Edward Barrow the man in charge, and he saw to it that McCarthy had a team that could reach a fourth straight world championship.

Trouble on the Diamond

Spring training began in St. Petersburg and was, as always, full of promise. Within a week, though, it became obvious something was ailing Gehrig. He was running poorly, he was not fielding balls with any assurance, and his hitting was worse than the year before. And while most sportswriters had previously held their critical opinions, eventually a report about Gehrig's health hit the *World-Telegraph*. Suddenly, the floodgates opened. Everyone started speculating that age had finally caught up with the Iron Horse.

McCarthy was also growing worried. He needed to let Gehrig be the judge of his own health and take a rest if needed. He made similar comments in the papers that spring.

By 1939, Gehrig had voluntarily benched himself after a poor showing during spring training. After 2,130 games, the Yankee legend was starting to slow down.

"I knew there was something seriously wrong with him," Bill Dickey recalled in the Tullius book *I'd Rather Be a Yankee*, "I didn't know what it was, but I knew it was serious.

"We were in the room one day . . . and Lou stumbled as he walked across the floor. I was reading a paper and looked up to what he had stumbled over, but there was nothing there. I was going to ask him what had happened, but he had a strange look on his face and I didn't say anything."

The season started with Gehrig at first, hitting fourth. In those first eight games, he managed only four hits and uncharacteristically committed two errors in just two games. After eight games, he had managed only four hits, he was dropped to fifth in the order, and it was clear that he was not improving. When the team had a day off on May 1 and traveled to Detroit, Gehrig spoke with Eleanor about quitting the team. He recalled the moment that decided it for him: "They don't think I can do it anymore. Maybe I can, maybe I can't, but they're talking about it, now, they're even writing about it. And when they're not talking, I can almost feel what they're thinking. Then I wish to God that they would talk—you know, say anything but sit there looking," Eleanor wrote in her memoir, *My Luke and I.*

"One day I made a routine play on a ground ball and [pitcher Johnny Murphy] Murph, [Joe] Gordon, and Dickey all gathered around me and patted me on the back. 'Great stop,' they all said together, and then I knew I was washed up. They meant to be kind, but if I was getting wholesale congratulations for making an ordinary stop, I knew it was time to fold," Gehrig remembered.

McCarthy recounted for the press what happened next.

"There was a knock on the door and Gehrig came in. He was troubled, I could see that.

" 'Joe,' he said, 'how much longer do you think I should stay in this game? When do you think I should get out?'

" 'Right now, Lou,' I said.

"He didn't say anything right away, just sat there. Then he said, 'Well, that's what I wanted to know.'

Gehrig in tears after fans attending Lou Gehrig Appreciation Day on July 4, 1939, honor him with a standing ovation

" 'That's what I think,' I said.

" 'That's the way I feel too,' he said. 'I'm not doing the ball club any good.'"

Gehrig's Last Season

The journalist Art Hill wrote in *I Don't Care If I Never Come Back*, "Gehrig trudged painfully up to the plate, carrying the lineup card without his name on it. It was one of the most moving moments in sports history, high drama of the sort you cannot make up."

The umpire was stunned to see Gehrig's name missing, and then the announcer called that Babe Dahlgren would instead be playing first base. There was a two-minute standing ovation for the Iron Horse, who ended a streak of 2,130 consecutive games played. It was an emotional moment.

McCarthy initially let it seem like Gehrig was getting a rest, but comments he made to several New York newspapers over the following days sealed his fate: Gehrig's playing days were over. Ed Barrow assured them that Gehrig would remain on salary for the remainder of the 1939 season and that he would stay in uniform as the team's captain.

Gehrig continued to travel with the team, shuffling out to home plate to hand over the lineup card to the umpire. The season became a farewell tour of sorts, whether it was officially called so or not. Many baseball greats of the day paused to shake Gehrig's hand.

A Grim Fate

People often speculate when Gehrig's disease took hold. It wasn't until 1989, in *Neurology*, a medical journal, that the University of Kentucky's Dr. Edward Kasarskis published his study that showed Gehrig's fall-off was traceable, leading the doctor to conclude that the disease began affecting Gehrig in 1937. Kasarskis saw many physical clues in *Rawhide*, meaning that poor health was affecting Gehrig between the 1937 and 1938 seasons.

On the team's next trip out of town, friends convinced Eleanor to have her husband examined by a group of medical experts. Together they arranged a visit to the renowned Mayo Clinic in Minnesota.

He spent six days at the clinic and was subjected to a battery of tests. The results were bleak. He had amyotrophic lateral sclerosis, a disease that destroys the myelin sheath that covers the body's nerve fibers. Without that protection, a scar forms and inhibits electric impulses to be carried, which prevents the body's nerves from working. It is a progressive disease that spreads from the limbs to the rest of the body over time. The doctor telephoned Eleanor with the news and gave it to her straight: Her husband had fewer than three years to live. Eleanor desperately researched the disease so she could be prepared to care for the ailing husband to whom she had been married for only five years.

Fond Farewells

After the diagnosis, Mayor Fiorello LaGuardia of New York City offered Gehrig a job as a member of the city's three-person parole board. Gehrig thought this was a good way for him to help the city, so he accepted the position. On train trips across the country, he was seen reading books in preparation. Eleanor spoke with the mayor privately and assured him she would notify him when her husband could no longer perform his duties.

When it became apparent to the Yankees that Gehrig would not be getting better, the notion of a Lou Gehrig Appreciation Day was conceived. Barrow scheduled it for July 4, between a doubleheader with the Washington Senators. The forty-minute ceremony, before 61,808 fans, was the first of its kind, with many old-time Yankee greats returning to the stadium to honor their teammate.

Many speeches were made, and a great number of gifts were bestowed on Gehrig, including one from his teammates—a wooden box shaped like home plate topped with a silver baseball.

When Gehrig spoke to the fans, he uttered some of the most memorable words spoken in the twentieth century. "Today, I consider myself to be the luckiest man on the face of this earth," Gehrig said during his farewell speech.

Even Babe Ruth showed up and threw his arms around Gehrig, showing the press that there remained no hard feelings between the legendary players.

Barrow also chose to honor Gehrig by retiring his number, 4, the first time a professional athlete's number was retired. Though it was only a decade after Barrow had introduced the numbers, they were already being closely associated with players, so it was a special honor.

Babe Ruth shares an emotional moment with his old friend on July 4, 1939, when the recently retired Gehrig was honored in a special ceremony at Yankee Stadium.

The 1939 Yankees stormed their way to another pennant and series, this time with Gehrig cheering from the dugout. The lineup that year is often considered to rival that of the 1927 Yankees as baseball's greatest.

A Civil Servant

By December 8, 1939, sportswriters announced that they had unanimously voted to waive the required waiting period and would induct Gehrig into the Baseball Hall of Fame that year.

To prepare for his new job on the parole board, Gehrig had to live within New York City's limits, so Eleanor sought a house that could be upgraded to anticipate the day when Gehrig needed a wheelchair. She found just such a house in the Riverdale section of the Bronx.

Each morning, starting in January 1940, Eleanor drove Gehrig to his job, which usually meant visiting inmates at prisons like Riker's Island or the Tombs and listening to their stories. He influenced many prisoners, including Rocco Barbella, later known as the boxer Rocky Graziano, who credited Gehrig with helping him get his life on track.

Gehrig managed to fulfill his duties for about a year and took them seriously, listening to each case and making a well-considered recommendation. After New Year's Day 1941, Eleanor told Mayor LaGuardia that Gehrig could no longer continue.

When he could, Gehrig visited Yankee Stadium, where he was mobbed by his colleagues. It was emotionally hard on Gehrig, but he enjoyed the familiar surroundings. Later

Gehrig sits with Eleanor while preparing for his new job on New York City's parole commission, shortly before being sworn in for the post in November 1939.

he commented that he had come to appreciate his teammates, something he had rarely had a chance to do while he was also in the game.

Great Courage

Gehrig and Eleanor often stayed inside their Bronx home, and they had a small dog named Yankee to keep them company. The home, though, became a magnet for a steady stream of visitors. Day by day, two servants tended to the house while Eleanor remained upstairs with her husband. Dr. Caldwell Esselstyn, a local physician, was sometimes asked by the Mayo Clinic to look after Gehrig.

Eleanor remained a touchstone to her husband, which explains why he said in his 1939 farewell speech, "When you have a wife who has been a tower of strength and shown more courage than you dreamed existed, that's the finest I know."

In turn, Eleanor later wrote of Gehrig in *My Luke and I*, "I would not have traded two minutes of the joy and the grief with that man for two decades of anything with another."

Visitors to the Gehrig home were a colorful bunch, including fellow teammate and best friend Bill Dickey, shortstop Frank Crosetti, and Ed Barrow and his wife, Fanny. Actress Tallulah Bankhead, who was moved when she heard Gehrig's farewell speech, had been corresponding with Gehrig ever since. When she came to New York to perform in a play called *The Little Foxes*, she finally met Gehrig and became a regular at the house.

Gehrig's 1939 Farewell Speech

"Fans, for the past two weeks you have been reading about the bad break I got. Yet today I consider myself the luckiest man on the face of this earth. I have been in ballparks for seventeen years and have never received anything but kindness and encouragement from you fans. Look at these grand men. Which of you wouldn't consider it the highlight of his career just to associate with them for even one day? Sure, I'm lucky. Who wouldn't consider it an honor to have known Jacob Ruppert? Also, the builder of baseball's greatest empire, Edward Barrow? To have spent six years with that wonderful little fellow, Miller Huggins? Then to have spent the next nine years with that outstanding leader, that smart student of psychology, the best manager in baseball today, Joe McCarthy? Sure, I'm lucky. When the New York Giants, a team you would give your right arm to beat, and vice versa, sends you a gift—that's something. When everybody down to the groundskeepers and those boys in white coats remember you with trophies—that's something.

When you have a wonderful mother-in-law who takes sides with you in squabbles with her own daughter—that's something. When you have a father and a mother who work all their lives so you can have an education and build your body— it's a blessing. When you have a wife who has been a tower of strength and shown more courage than you dreamed existed—that's the finest I know. So I close in saying that I may have had a tough break, but I have an awful lot to live for."

Gehrig's mother, Christina, however, rarely came by. In fact, she stayed away. Finally, in Gehrig's last weeks, Eleanor dispatched two close friends to bring Christina to her son. She arrived quietly, visited with him once, and never returned.

In the final weeks, Gehrig remained in bed, sipping orange juice and milkshakes, held by his wife's loving hand. His mind remained alert, but he could no longer move on his own. Even breathing became difficult, so he slept much of the time.

On the evening of June 2, 1941—the sixteenth anniversary of Gehrig replacing Wally

Pipp in the lineup—Gehrig passed away at 10:10 PM. "The most beatified expression instantly spread over Lou's face," Eleanor wrote in her memoir, *My Luke and I*, "And I knew the precise moment he had gone."

Gehrig's Legacy

In keeping with his quiet, unassuming manner, Gehrig did not want a large funeral. It was a quiet, small ceremony, lasting for a mere eight minutes. He was cremated, and his remains were buried at Kensico Cemetery in Valhalla, New York. A month later, a memorial was erected in center field at Yankee Stadium. Gehrig would never be forgotten.

Now Gehrig's legend continued to shine. Samuel Goldwyn, head of MGM Studios, made a movie of Gehrig's life after being shown newsreel footage of the player in action. Gehrig's journalist friend Fred Lieb helped to shape the story that used only some of the facts of Gehrig's life and embellished the rest. Gary Cooper, the stoic leading man, was cast as

Yankee players, politicians, and Eleanor Gehrig look on as former teammate Bill Dickey (*left*) and manager Joe McCarthy unveil a monument to Gehrig in Yankee Stadium on July 6, 1941.

Gehrig with the much younger Teresa Wright cast as Eleanor. Dickey and Ruth played themselves to add some authenticity to the film.

Pride of the Yankees, released in 1942, was a smash hit and remains a springtime staple on television. Cooper, when he visited troops during World War II, was surprised by requests to recreate Gehrig's famous farewell speech. At first, he could not recall all the words, but he quickly relearned them, entertaining troops throughout Europe.

Gehrig's birthplace was memorialized on August 21, 1953, when a plaque was erected with his mother in attendance. It was her final public appearance.

Phi Delta Theta, Gehrig's fraternity at Columbia University, honored his memory with an annual award in 1955. The Lou Gehrig Award has since been given to baseball players who best exemplify the character of Gehrig, both on and off the field.

Climax, a 1956 anthology series, retold Gehrig's story in one installment. Wendell Long played Gehrig, and Jean Hagen, best known for *Singin' in the Rain*, played Eleanor.

In 1968, the *Sporting News* named the 100 greatest baseball players of all time as professional baseball celebrated its 100th birthday. Gehrig placed sixth on the list. One year later, legend Mickey Mantle retired from the Yankees and had his own appreciation day. Around that time, he said, "I never knew how

Professional Career Statistics

Year	Tm	G	AB	R	H	2B	3B	HR	RBI	SB	CS	BB	SO	BA	OBP	SLG
1923	NYY	13	26	6	11	4	1	1	9	0	0	2	5	.423	.464	.769
1924	NYY	10	12	2	6	1	0	0	5	0	0	1	3	.500	.538	.583
1925	NYY	126	437	73	129	23	10	20	68	6	3	46	49	.295	.365	.531
1926	NYY	155	572	135	179	47	20	16	112	6	5	105	73	.313	.420	.549
1927	NYY	155	584	149	218	52	18	47	175	10	8	109	84	.373	.474	.765
1928	NYY	154	562	139	210	47	13	27	142	4	11	95	69	.374	.467	.648
1929	NYY	154	553	127	166	32	10	35	126	4	4	122	68	.300	.431	.584
1930	NYY	154	581	143	220	42	17	41	174	12	14	101	63	.379	.473	.721
1931	NYY	155	619	163	211	31	15	46	184	17	12	117	56	.341	.446	.662
1932	NYY	156	596	138	208	42	9	34	151	4	11	108	38	.349	.451	.621
1933	NYY	152	593	138	198	41	12	32	139	9	13	92	42	.334	.424	.605
1934	NYY	154	579	128	210	40	6	49	165	9	5	109	31	.363	.465	.706
1935	NYY	149	535	125	176	26	10	30	119	8	7	132	38	.329	.466	.583
1936	NYY	155	579	167	205	37	7	49	152	3	4	130	46	.354	.478	.696
1937	NYY	157	569	138	200	37	9	37	159	4	3	127	49	.351	.473	.643
1938	NYY	157	576	115	170	32	6	29	114	6	1	107	75	.295	.410	.523
1939	NYY	8	28	2	4	0	0	0	1	0	0	5	1	.143	.273	.143
17 Seasons		2,164	8,001	1,888	2,721	534	163	493	1,995	102	101	1,508	790	.340	.447	.632

Year	Tm	G	AB	R	H	2B	3B	HR	RBI	SB	CS	BB	SO	BA	OBP	SLG
162 Game Avg			599	141	204	40	12	37	149	8	8	113	59	.340	.447	.632
Career High		157	619	167	220	52	20	49	184	17	14	132	84	.379	.478	.765

Postseason Batting

Year	Rnd	Tm	Opp	G	AB	R	H	2B	3B	HR	RBI	BB	SO	BA	OBP	SLG	SB
1926	WS	NYY	STL	7	23	1	8	2	0	0	4	5	4	.348	.464	.435	0
1927	WS	NYY	PIT	4	13	2	4	2	2	0	4	3	3	.308	.437	.769	0
1928	WS	NYY	STL	4	11	5	6	1	0	4	9	6	0	.545	.706	1.727	0
1932	WS	NYY	CHC	4	17	9	9	1	0	3	8	2	1	.529	.579	1.118	0
1936	WS	NYY	NYG	6	24	5	7	1	0	2	7	3	2	.292	.370	.583	0
1937	WS	NYY	NYG	5	17	4	5	1	1	1	3	5	4	.294	.455	.647	0
1938	WS	NYY	CHC	4	14	4	4	0	0	0	0	2	3	.286	.375	.286	0
7 World Series				34	119	30	43	8	3	10	35	26	17	.361	.476	.731	0

Statistics Glossary

Year: Year in which the season occurred; Rnd: Round; Tm: Team played for; G: Games played; AB: At bats; R: Runs scored; H: Hits; 2B: Doubles; 3B: Triples; HR: Home runs; RBI: Runs batted in; SB: Stolen bases; CS: Caught stealing (were counted in the AL after 1919 and after 1950 in the NL); BB: Base on balls, or walks; SO: Strikeouts (are available hit and miss between 1882 and 1912, but are available for all other seasons); BA: Batting average H/AB; OBP: On-base percentage (H+BB+HBP)/(AB+BB+SF+HBP); SLG: Slugging percentage TB/AB.

Stats source: http://www.baseball-reference.com/about/bat_glossary.shtml

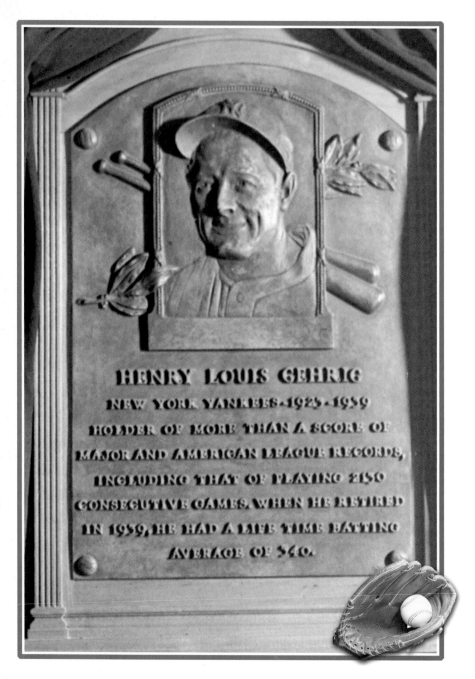

HENRY LOUIS GEHRIG
NEW YORK YANKEES · 1923 · 1939
HOLDER OF MORE THAN A SCORE OF
MAJOR AND AMERICAN LEAGUE RECORDS,
INCLUDING THAT OF PLAYING 2130
CONSECUTIVE GAMES. WHEN HE RETIRED
IN 1939, HE HAD A LIFE TIME BATTING
AVERAGE OF .340.

In a special election, Lou Gehrig was inducted into the Baseball Hall of Fame in 1939, and this plaque was installed there to honor his achievements.

someone dying could say he was the luckiest man in the world. But now I understand."

In 1976, Eleanor released her memoir, which recounted their love story and Gehrig's tragic death. The well-reviewed book was later used as the basis for a television movie in 1977.

Claire Ruth, who lost the Babe to cancer in 1948, reconciled her friendship with Eleanor Gehrig and the two were fixtures at Yankee Stadium during Old Timers Day events. Eleanor's last public appearance was in 1983, and she passed away in 1984 at the age of seventy-nine. She was buried beside Gehrig.

In 1989, Lou Gehrig became the fourth baseball player to be remembered on a first-class stamp, a fitting tribute to an American role model.

LOU GEHRIG *TIMELINE*

⚾	**June 19** **1903**	Henry Louis Gehrig II is born.
⚾	**1921**	Gehrig is awarded a scholarship to Columbia University.
⚾	**1922**	Gehrig becomes a football fullback as a sophomore at Columbia.
⚾	**1923**	Paul Krichell scouts and signs Gehrig in less than a week. Gehrig works with the Yankees but is sent to Hartford, Connecticut, for minor-league training.
⚾	**Sept.** **1923**	Gehrig is called up to the majors in September. He hits .423 in 26 at-bats.
⚾	**1925**	Gehrig's first full season with the Yankees.
⚾	**1926**	Gehrig leads the American League with 20 triples.
⚾	**1927**	Gehrig becomes the American League's Most Valuable Player (MVP).
⚾	**1931**	With 184 runs batted in (RBIs) Gehrig hits the American League record—topped only by Hack Wilson's National League record.

⚾	**1932**	Gehrig hits four home runs in a game, a modern-era record.
⚾	**1933**	Gehrig marries Eleanor Grace Twitchell.
⚾	**1934**	Gehrig sets the record with the prestigious Triple Crown in batting with a .363 average, 49 home runs, and 165 RBIs.
⚾	**1936**	Gehrig leads the American League in home runs and runs scored.
⚾	**1938**	Experiencing the first signs of amyotrophic lateral sclerosis, Gehrig's batting average plummets.
⚾	**1939**	Gehrig removes himself from the Yankee lineup, ending his streak of 2,130 consecutive games. By December of that year he is inducted into the Baseball Hall of Fame.
⚾	**1940**	Gehrig is sworn in as member of New York City's parole board.
⚾	**1941**	Lou Gehrig dies at age thirty-seven.

Glossary

barnstorming   A common practice in the first half of the twentieth century. Baseball players would travel from town to town across the United States playing two or three games a day.

base on balls   Commonly referred to as a walk; when a batter receives four pitches that are out of the strike zone, he is awarded first base.

batter's box   The area beside home plate in which the batter must stand while at bat. The batter cannot leave his position in the batter's box after the pitcher comes to the set position or begins his windup.

batting average   The number of at bats divided by the number of hits; a .300 batting average (180 hits in 600 at bats) is a standard goal.

chronic   Marked by frequent recurrence; habitual.

doubleheader   Two games played in the same day, one after the other.

double steal   A play in which two players, each on a base, both attempt to steal the next base, usually rattling the opposing team.

dugout   The area reserved for players and other team members when they are not actively engaged on the playing field.

frugal   A characteristic of using resources economically.

inept   Lacking in aptitude; incompetent.

jeopardize   To expose to danger or risk.

naïve   Marked by innocence, or a lack of experience or skill.

runs batted in (RBIs)   The number of runs a batter drives home via a hit, sacrifice bunt or fly, walk, fielder's choice, or error.

segregate   To separate some people apart from others based on their race, ethnicity, or religion.

stoic   A characteristic of not showing emotion; impassive; indifferent.

strike out   When a batter swings and misses three pitches, receives three pitches within the strike zone without swinging, or a combination of the two. The batter is declared out.

World Series   The championship baseball series matching the winners of the American League and the National League. The series is preceded by divisional and league championship series in each league. The World Series is a best-of-seven affair that takes place in October and has been held annually since 1903 (except in 1904 and 1994).

For More Information

Major League Baseball
245 Park Avenue, 31st Floor
New York, NY 10167
(212) 931-7800
Web site: http://www.mlb.com

The National Baseball Hall of Fame
    and Museum
25 Main Street
P.O. Box 590
Cooperstown, NY 13326
(888) 425-5633
Web site: http://www.baseballhalloffame.org

Society for American Baseball Records
812 Huron Road, Suite 719
Cleveland, OH 44115
(216) 575-0500
Web site: http://www.sabr.org

Yankee Stadium
161st Street and River Avenue
Bronx, NY 10452
Web site: http://newyork.yankees.mlb.com

Web Sites

Due to the changing nature of Internet links, the Rosen Publishing Group, Inc., has developed an online list of Web sites related to the subject of this book. This site is updated regularly. Please use this link to access the list:

http://www.rosenlinks.com/bhf/lgeh

For Further Reading

Gehrig, Eleanor, and Joseph Durso. *My Luke and I*. New York: Thomas Y. Crowell Company, 1976.

Graham, Frank. *Lou Gehrig, A Quiet Hero*. New York: G.P. Putnam's Sons, 1942.

Robinson, Ray. *Iron Horse: Lou Gehrig in His Time*. New York: W.W. Norton & Company, 1990.

Ruscoe, Michael, ed. *Baseball: A Treasury of Art and Literature*. Southport, CT: Hugh Lauter Levin Associates Inc., 1993.

Tofel, Richard J. *A Legend in the Making*. Chicago: Ivan R. Dee, 2002.

Ward, Geoffrey C., and Ken Burns. *Baseball: An Illustrated History*. New York: Alfred A. Knopf, 1994.

Bibliography

Anderson, Dave, Murray Chass, Robert Creamer, and Harold Rosenthal. *The Yankees: The Four Fabulous Eras of Baseball's Most Famous Team.* New York: Random House, 1979.

Cataneo, David. *Peanuts and Crackerjack.* Nashville, TN: Rutledge Hill Press, 1991.

Chadwick, Bruce, and David M. Spindel. *The Bronx Bombers.* New York: Abbeville Press, 1992.

Chadwin, Dean. *Those Damn Yankees.* New York: Verso Books, 1999.

Dickson, Paul. *Baseball's Greatest Quotations.* New York: Edward Burlingame Books, 1991.

Gehrig, Eleanor, and Joseph Durso. *My Luke and I.* New York: Thomas Y. Crowell Company, 1976.

Graham, Frank. *Lou Gehrig, A Quiet Hero.* New York: G.P. Putnam's Sons, 1942.

Honig, Donald. *Baseball: When the Grass Was Real.* New York: Coward, McCann, & Geoghegan, Inc., 1975.

Hubler, Richard. *Lou Gehrig: The Iron Horse of Baseball.* Boston: Houghton Mifflin Company, 1941.

Robinson, Ray. *Iron Horse: Lou Gehrig in His Time.* New York: W.W. Norton & Company, 1990.

Ruscoe, Michael, ed. *Baseball: A Treasury of Art and Literature.* Southport, CT: Hugh Lauter Levin Associates Inc., 1993.

Sporting News. *Baseball's Greatest Players.* St. Louis, MO: Sporting News, 1998.

Sugar, Bert Randolph. *Rain Delays.* New York: St. Martin's Press, 1990.

Thorn, John. *A Century of Baseball Lore.* New York: Hart Publishing Company, Inc., 1974.

Tofel, Richard J. *A Legend in the Making.* Chicago: Ivan R. Dee, 2002.

Tullius, John. *I'd Rather Be a Yankee.* New York: Macmillan Publishing Company, 1986.

Wallace, Joseph, ed. *The Baseball Anthology.* New York: Harry N. Abrams, Inc., 1994.

Ward, Geoffrey C., and Ken Burns. *Baseball: An Illustrated History.* New York: Alfred A. Knopf, 1994.

Index

About the Author

Robert Greenberger spends his days as a senior editor at DC Comics. By night, he writes books on all sorts of subjects, from *Star Trek* novels to nonfiction. His great passion is baseball. He makes his home in Connecticut with his wife Deb and children Katie and Robbie.

Photo Credits

Cover, pp. 78, 86, 96 © AP/Wide World Photos; pp. 4, 9, 11, 18, 22, 27, 29, 32–33, 36, 43, 45, 48, 51, 57, 60, 63, 69, 74, 81, 88, 93 © Bettmann/ Corbis; pp. 6, 90 © Corbis; p. 13 © Michael Maslan Historic Photographs/Corbis; pp. 39, 41 © Underwood & Underwood/Corbis; p. 71 © TimePix.

Editor

Joann Jovinelly

Series Design and Layout

Geri Giordano